Lions

Patricia Kendell

HODDER
Wayland

An imprint of Hodder Children's Books

in the wild

Chimpanzees Dolphins Elephants
Lions Polar Bears Tigers

© 2002 White-Thomson Publishing Ltd

Produced for Hodder Wayland by White-Thomson Publishing Ltd

Editor: Kay Barnham
Designer: Tim Mayer
Consultant: David Macdonald, Director of Oxford University's
   Wildlife Conservation Unit
Language Consultant: Norah Granger, Senior Lecturer in Primary
   Education at the University of Brighton.

Published in Great Britain in 2002 by Hodder Wayland,
an imprint of Hodder Children's Books.
First published in paperback in 2002

The right of Patricia Kendell to be identified as the author of this
Work has been asserted by her in accordance with the Copyright,
Designs and Patents Act 1988.

Photograph acknowledgements:
BBC Natural History Unit 21 (Keith Scholey); Bruce Coleman 3
(fourth), 7, 18, 29 (Johnny Johnson); Ecoscene 3 (third), 19 (Kjell
Sandved); NHPA 3 (first), 10 (Rich Kirchner), 14 (Nigel Dennis),
16 (Gerard Lacz), 20 (Nigel Dennis), 24 (Ann & Steve Toon),
32 (Rich Kirchner); Oxford Scientific Films 5 (Stan Oslinski), 12
(Adrian Bailey), 17 (Owen Newnan); Papilio 1, 15, 23, 26;
Science Photo Library 3 (second), 9 Gregory Dimijian), 11 (Tim
Davis), 22 (Gregory Dimijian), 25 (Tim Davis); Staffan Widstrand
28; Still Pictures 4 (Muriel Nicolotti), 6 & 8 (M & C Denis-Huot)

British Library Cataloguing in Publication Data
Kendell, Patricia
   Lions. - (In the wild)
   1. Lions
   I. Title
   599.7'57

ISBN: 0 7502 4002 4

Printed and bound in Hong Kong

Hodder Children's Books
A division of Hodder Headline Limited
338 Euston Road, London NW1 3BH

Produced in association with WWF-UK.
WWF-UK registered charity number 1081247.
A company limited by guarantee number 4016725.
Panda device © 1986 WWF ® WWF registered trademark owner.

Contents

Where lions live

Lions live in the grasslands and woodlands of Africa.
A few lions live in forests in India.

4

The lion is one of the biggest and most powerful members of the cat family. A female lion is called a lioness.

Baby lions

Baby lions are called cubs. These cubs were
born in a safe, secret den made by their mother.

If the mother senses danger,
she moves them to another
safe place.

Looking after the cubs

The cubs drink milk from their mother as often as they can to grow big and strong.

The lioness cares for the cubs.
Here, she **grooms** them to keep them clean.

Joining the family

When the cubs are older, the lioness takes them to meet the **pride**. The lionesses help each other to look after all the cubs.

The cubs' father does not take care of them. His job is to **defend** the lionesses and cubs from other lions.

Growing up

The cubs have a lot to learn about how to find food, keep clean and stay out of danger.

Playing games helps them to learn the skills they will need to survive.

Hunting

Lionesses **stalk** their **prey**. This lioness has spotted a herd of zebra. She is ready to attack.

It is nearly night-time and this lioness is ready to go hunting. It is cooler now and she can see well in the dark.

Eating ...

After a kill, the lion eats first. Then it is the turn of the lionesses and cubs.

This lion is using his rough tongue to clean himself after eating.

drinking ...

Lions need to drink every day. They lap the water with their tongues, just like cats that live in our homes.

...and sleeping

After a good meal, lions will sleep
for up to 20 hours a day.

Leaving home

Male cubs have to leave the pride when
they are two years old. From now on,
this cub will have to look after himself.

At first, they are not very good at hunting – and are often hungry. They will steal meat killed by other animals.

Finding a mate

When a male cub is fully grown, he has to find a lioness to be his **mate**, so they can have cubs of their own.

This lion is watching over his mate. He is making sure that other lions stay away from her.

'King of the beasts'

Only one lion can be the head of the pride. He must be strong enough to fight off all the other lions.

This lion's mane of hair makes him look big and powerful.

Lions in danger

Today, people need more space to grow food.

They also build roads across lions' land.
Lions have less space in which
to live and hunt.

Helping lions to survive

Some lions now live on **reserves**.
Tourists have come to see this lion in the wild.

These lions are safe, happy and free.

Further information

Find out more about how we can help lions in the future.

ORGANISATIONS TO CONTACT

WWF-UK
Panda House, Weyside Park,
Godalming, Surrey GU7 1XR
Tel: 01483 426444

Care for the Wild International
1 Ashfolds, Horsham Road,
Rusper, West Sussex RH12 4QX
Tel: 01293 871596

Born Free Foundation
3 Grove House, Foundry Lane,
Horsham, Sussex RH13 5PL
Tel: 01403 240170

BOOKS

Watch us play: Miela Ford, Greenwillow 1998.

Lions: (First discovery books):
Jean-Philippe Chabot, Scholastic 2000.

Lion: King of the Beasts: (Animal close-ups): Christine Denis-Huot, Charlesbridge Publishing 2000.

The Big Cats: Lions, Tigers and Leopards: Jennifer Urquhart, National Geographic Society 1996.

The Lion Family Book: Angelika Hofer, North South Books 1995.

WEBSITES

Most young children will need adult help when visiting websites. Those below have child-friendly pages that could be bookmarked.

http://www.lionresearch.org
Information for adults and older pupils.

http://www.asiatic-lion.org
Information about Asiatic lions and their conservation with photographic sequences.

http://www.bornfree.org.uk
News and information about a range of animals and how to 'adopt' animals in order to help their survival.

http://www.careforthewild.org
Information about how to protect a range of animals against cruelty and exploitation, with factsheets for more able readers.

Visit learn.co.uk for more resources

learn.co.uk
from *The Guardian*

Glossary

defend – to protect or look after.

groom – to clean the coat of an animal.

mate – a lion has a lioness for a mate; they make babies together.

prey – an animal hunted by another animal for food.

pride – a group of lions.

stalk – to creep up on.

reserves – safe places where wild animals can live freely.

Index